4/09

Queens and Princesses

QUEEN
Elizabeth I
OF ENGLAND

by Robert Kraske

Consultant:

Eric J. Carlson, PhD

Professor of History, Gustavus Adolphus College

St. Peter, Minnesota

Capstone *press*

Mankato, Minnesota

Snap Books are published by Capstone Press,
151 Good Counsel Drive, P.O. Box 669, Mankato, Minnesota 56002.
www.capstonepress.com

Library of Congress Cataloging-in-Publication Data
Kraske, Robert.
    Queen Elizabeth I of England / by Robert Kraske.
    p. cm. — (Snap Books. Queens and princesses)
    Includes bibliographical references and index.
    Summary: "Describes the life and death of Queen Elizabeth I of England" —
Provided by publisher.
    ISBN-13: 978-1-4296-2311-7 (hardcover)
    ISBN-10: 1-4296-2311-X (hardcover)
    1. Elizabeth I, Queen of England, 1533–1603 — Juvenile literature. 2. Great
Britain — History — Elizabeth, 1558–1603 — Juvenile literature. 3. Queens —
Great Britain — Biography — Juvenile literature. I. Title.
DA355.K73 2009
942.05'5092 — dc22   2008030937

Editorial Credits:

Kathryn Clay, editor; Bobbi J. Wyss, book designer; Juliette Peters, set designer;
    Wanda Winch, photo researcher

Photo Credits:

Art Resource, N.Y./ Réunion des Musées Nationaux, 27; The Bridgeman Art Library International/Hatfield
House, Hertfordshire, UK /The Knot Garden and the Old Palace, from the north-east (photo), 10; The
Bridgeman Art Library International/Private Collection, © Look and Learn/Elizabeth I - (1533-1603) The
Warrior Queen (gouache on paper), Doughty, C.L. (1913-85), 25; The Bridgeman Art Library International/
Yale Center for British Art, Paul Mellon Collection, USA, / Robert Dudley (1532-88) 1st Earl of Leicester,
c.1560s (oil on panel), Meulen, or Muelen, Steven van der (fl.1543-68), 21; Corbis/Fine Art Photographic
Library, 18; Getty Images Inc./Hulton Archive, 11; Getty Images Inc./Hulton Archive/Edward Gooch, 7;
Getty Images Inc./Hulton Archive/Stock Montage, 13; Getty Images Inc./Popperfoto, 6; Getty Images Inc./
The Bridgeman Art Library/After Taddeo Zuccari, 17; Getty Images Inc./The Bridgeman Art Library/
Arthur Hopkins, 9; Getty Images Inc./The Bridgeman Art Library/English School, 5, 29; Getty Images Inc./
The Bridgeman Art Library/John Byam Liston Shaw, 12; Getty Images Inc./The Bridgeman Art Library/
Sarah Countess of Essex, 19; North Wind Picture Archives, 23, 24; "Princess Elizabeth at Woodstock."
Engraved by R. W. Smart from a design by H. Fradelle. Image courtesy of Katherine D. Harris, "Forget Me
Not: A Hypertextual Archive of Ackermann's 19th-Century Literary Annual", http://www.orgs.muohio.edu/
anthologies/FMN/Index.htm, 14; SuperStock, Inc./National Portrait Gallery, London, cover

Essential content terms are **bold** and are defined at the bottom of the page where
they first appear.

1 2 3 4 5 6 14 13 12 11 10 09

Table of Contents

1 Coronation DAY

On January 14, 1559, a light snow fell on London streets. The cold could not dampen the spirits of the cheering crowd. Thousands of people waved flags and banners to honor their new queen.

"God save your grace!" the crowd called to Elizabeth Tudor, who would be crowned queen the next day. "God save you all! I thank you with all my heart!" she called in return.

Elizabeth rode through town in a chair carried by her guards. She wore a gown of gold cloth under a crimson robe lined with ermine fur. A thousand riders on prancing horses followed. Elizabeth listened politely as street performers gave speeches and choirs sang.

At age 25, Elizabeth Tudor was crowned queen of England.

The next day, Elizabeth went to Westminster Abbey. English kings and queens had been crowned at this historic church for 500 years. Today it was Elizabeth's turn. Though she had been queen since her sister's death in November 1558, today was her official **coronation**.

Princes, dukes, and other nobles watched as St. Edward's crown was placed on her red-gold hair. The crown, covered in gold and pearls, weighed 7 pounds (3 kilograms). In addition to the heavy crown, Elizabeth wore several layers of clothing and a royal robe. She paid little attention to the uncomfortable clothes. After all, she could hardly believe this was happening.

Nearly five years earlier, Elizabeth's life was very different. Her sister, Mary, had locked her away in the Tower of London. In that cold prison, Elizabeth had very little food and worried about her fate every day. But now Mary was dead, and Elizabeth was England's new queen.

Large crowds greeted their new queen, Elizabeth I.

coronation — the ceremony in which a king or queen is crowned

TOWER OF LONDON

William the Conqueror began construction of the Tower of London in 1078 to protect London from invaders. The oldest part of the tower is known as the White Tower. Royal prisoners, like Elizabeth, were jailed here.

Other parts of the tower were used as royal palaces. It was tradition for future kings and queens to spend a night in the tower before their coronations.

Now, the tower is a popular London tourist attraction. Visitors are able to see where Elizabeth was imprisoned. They might also see the Crown Jewels, which have been kept at the tower since 1303.

2

THE YOUNG
Princess

Elizabeth was born to King Henry VIII and Anne Boleyn on September 7, 1533. Henry had wanted a son to be his **heir** and was disappointed by Elizabeth's birth. Everyone thought the baby would be a boy. Announcements had already been printed to declare the birth of the new prince.

Anne Boleyn worried about having a daughter instead of a son. Anne was Henry's second wife. He divorced his first wife when she was unable to produce a son. If Anne had a boy, it would secure her place as queen. She worried that Henry might divorce her because she didn't have a son.

Henry VIII secretly married Anne Boleyn on January 15, 1533.

heir — someone who will become king or queen when the current ruler dies

YOUNG ELIZABETH'S TRAGEDY

Like most royal children of that time, Elizabeth did not grow up in the same castle as her parents. Still a baby, she was sent to live at Hatfield Royal Palace near London. There, nurses and servants took care of her. Though Elizabeth rarely saw her mother, Anne did not forget about her daughter. She sent Elizabeth fancy silk dresses and hats. At night, Elizabeth's nurses placed her in a golden cradle covered in ermine fur.

Just before Elizabeth turned 3 years old, the fancy clothes stopped arriving. Soon all her clothes were too small and worn thin. Though Elizabeth didn't know it at the time, her mother had been executed for **treason**. Less than one month later, her father was already planning his marriage to Jane Seymour.

Elizabeth enjoyed walking in the gardens of Hatfield Royal Palace.

treason — the act of betraying one's country

KING HENRY'S WIVES

Anne Boleyn was King Henry VIII's second wife. But Henry had many more wives after Anne. In fact, Henry was married six times.

Henry's first wife, Catherine of Aragon, gave birth to Princess Mary in 1516. Catherine and Henry wanted a son who would become the next king of England. When this didn't happen, Henry asked the Roman Catholic Church to grant him a divorce from Catherine.

The leader of the Catholic Church, the pope, refused. Divorce was against the teachings of the Church. Henry cut ties with the pope and the Catholic Church. With the help of Parliament, he set up the Church of England and was declared its leader. He divorced Catherine and married Anne Boleyn. Shortly after Elizabeth's birth, Henry lost interest in Anne. He **annulled** their marriage. Henry then accused Anne of treason and had her beheaded.

Henry's third wife, Jane Seymour, gave birth to Prince Edward in 1537. She died shortly after his birth. After her death, Henry VIII married three more times. None of the marriages produced another child.

Henry and his wives (clockwise from top): Anne of Cleaves, Catherine Howard, Anne Boleyn, Catherine of Aragon, Catherine Parr, and Jane Seymour.

annul — to cancel or end legally

A ROYAL EDUCATION

As a child, Elizabeth was too busy studying to notice her father's many marriages. She was smart and enjoyed learning. Tutors considered her a perfect student. She did well with mathematics, geography, and astronomy. She also learned to read several languages including Latin, Greek, French, and Italian.

When her studies were complete, Elizabeth danced at court with young nobles. On warm days, she spent hours walking in her gardens. Elizabeth also rode after deer on Hatfield's grounds. She was skilled with a crossbow and enjoyed long afternoon hunts.

A SHORT REIGN

When King Henry VIII died in 1547, Prince Edward took over the throne. The young prince was only 9 years old. Six years later, Edward died from smallpox. Elizabeth's older sister, Mary, became England's new queen.

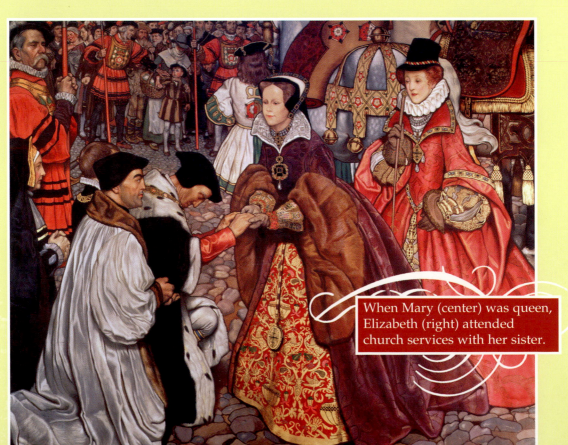

When Mary (center) was queen, Elizabeth (right) attended church services with her sister.

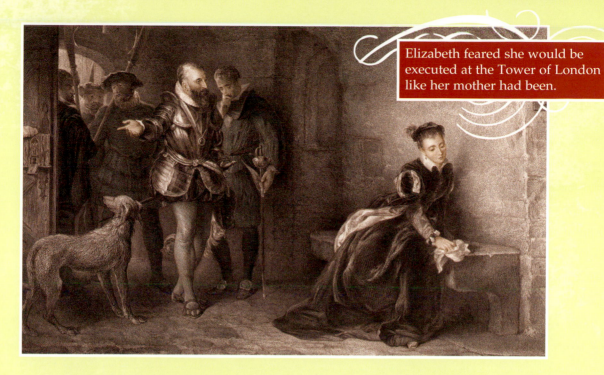

Elizabeth feared she would be executed at the Tower of London like her mother had been.

Queen Mary believed in the Catholic faith. Protestants, she said, were **heretics**. They did not follow the Roman Catholic Church's teachings. She ordered convicted heretics to be killed. Because more than 300 people died under Mary's reign, the people called her "Bloody Mary."

Elizabeth had grown up following the Protestant religion. She did not want to be a Catholic, but she attended services to make Mary happy. Still, Mary suspected her younger sister was practicing the Protestant religion in secret. Then something happened to convince Mary. In 1554, knight Thomas Wyatt began a revolt to place Elizabeth on the throne. Wyatt was a Protestant and disagreed with Mary's laws on religion. Elizabeth, who was only 20 years old, was charged with taking part in the plot. Mary ordered her sister sent to the Tower of London, the state prison.

Was Elizabeth about to be beheaded as her mother had been? She wrote to her sister and pleaded her innocence. But the letters went unread.

heretic — someone whose views are different from those of a particular region or unacceptable to people in authority

PRISONER IN HER OWN HOME

No proof of Elizabeth's participation in Wyatt's plot was ever found. Wyatt himself insisted on her innocence up until his execution. Two months after Elizabeth entered the Tower of London, she was released.

Though no longer living in the prison, Elizabeth was still closely guarded at a small house in Woodstock. The house had only four rooms. The roof leaked, and the air was cold. There were no fields for Elizabeth to ride after deer. Few books were in the house, and Elizabeth's requests for more were ignored.

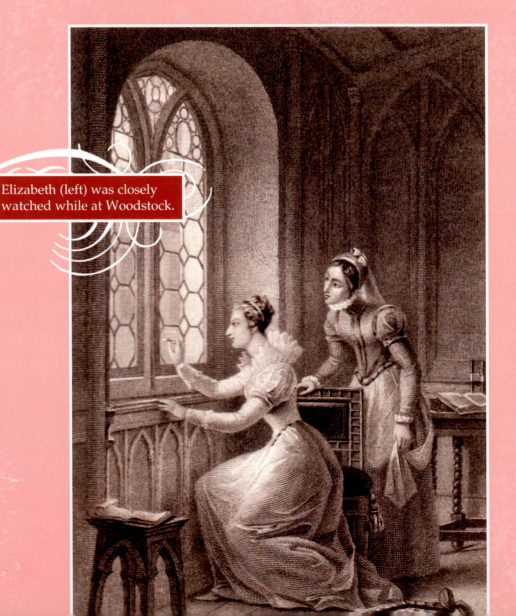

Elizabeth (left) was closely watched while at Woodstock.

Elizabeth was eventually allowed to return to Hatfield Royal Palace but not without several of Mary's guards to watch her. Elizabeth continued to maintain her innocence, but Mary did not trust her sister.

ELIZABETH'S TURN

After four years under house arrest, Elizabeth was suddenly granted her freedom in November 1558. As Elizabeth read a Greek Bible under an oak tree at Hatfield, a royal horseman galloped up. Kneeling before her, he reported that Queen Mary had died. As proof, he presented Mary's coronation ring. Elizabeth was now queen of England.

"This is the Lord's doing, and it is marvelous in our eyes."

Elizabeth quoting Psalm 118 after her sister's death

3

Elizabeth's
RULE

After her coronation, Elizabeth spent most days in Whitehall Palace, where her parents had married. Of the royal family's 60 castles and 50 houses, Whitehall was the largest. It covered 23 acres (9 hectares) and had more than 1,500 rooms. Brightly colored tapestries and woodcarvings decorated the large halls. Outside the palace were tennis courts and a bowling green.

Elizabeth was known for her collection of fancy dresses and jewels.

LIFE AS QUEEN

Elizabeth's days began early. Her maids curled her hair and dressed her slender body in heavy layers of clothes. Her royal attire was made up of a gown, petticoat, skirt, and lace ruff behind her neck. She covered herself in jewels, rings, and ropes of pearls.

Once she was dressed, servants applied thick makeup to Elizabeth's face. Her cheeks were scarred after having smallpox in 1562. A layer of egg whites and powdered eggshell left her face white against her red-gold hair. She also carried a bottle of perfume with her. Baths were rare at this time. The crowded courts often smelled of unwashed bodies. Elizabeth used the perfume to cover up the strong odors.

To relax from her duties as queen, Elizabeth played cards or chess with her ladies. They always made sure the queen won. She also played her lute and attended tennis matches. One of Elizabeth's favorite pastimes was going to the theater. She was fond of William Shakespeare's plays.

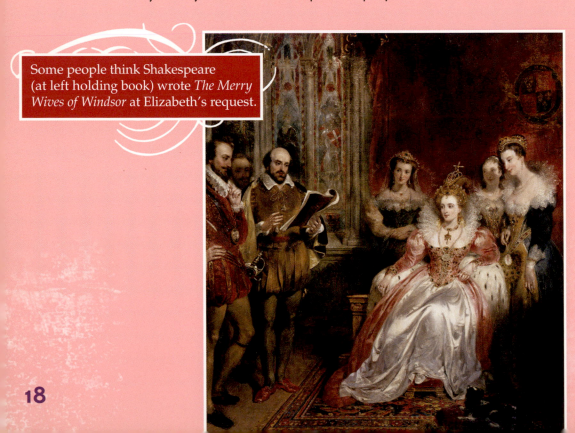

Some people think Shakespeare (at left holding book) wrote *The Merry Wives of Windsor* at Elizabeth's request.

A TRAVELING SHOW

In summer, Elizabeth and her court left the heat and smells of crowded London. A caravan of wagons and packhorses carried her dresses, jewels, and bed to nearby towns and villages. Nobles and servants followed.

During these trips, peasants saw her dressed in satin gowns covered with gems. She listened to their problems and roared with laughter at their jokes. After her visits, Elizabeth wept and made a great show of sadness about leaving. She was friendly with her subjects, but she always maintained her queenly manner.

As queen, Elizabeth planned to make England a Protestant country once again. This was the religion she had grown up practicing. Church of England services would be held in English instead of Latin. The Bible could now be read in English. People were allowed to celebrate the Catholic religion privately if they chose. But everyone more than 16 years old had to attend Church of England services on Sundays. Those who did not attend had to pay a fine.

Elizabeth received constant advice from Parliament and her Privy Council. This group of personal advisors urged Elizabeth to marry. They wanted her to produce an heir to the throne. Kings and princes from other countries offered marriage proposals. Elizabeth refused each proposal. Marriage would mean sharing her royal power, and she wasn't ready for that.

Elizabeth refused to name an heir. She worried that naming a successor might cause a revolt. She reminded her council that as long as she was living, she would be queen of England.

"I would rather be a beggar and single than a queen and married."

Elizabeth responding to questions about a possible marriage

ELIZABETH'S ONE TRUE LOVE?

For many years, Elizabeth's closest companion was Robert Dudley. Dudley was tall, handsome, and charming. They often went on deer hunts or spent long afternoons talking. They danced together at court. He sent her love letters and proposed marriage. But still, Elizabeth resisted his proposals. Even though she loved him, she was not ready to share her crown.

When Dudley died in 1588, he left Elizabeth diamonds and pearls. In a final letter, Dudley thanked her for the medicine she had given him. She kept this last letter in a pearl-covered box at her bedside.

Was Robert Dudley Elizabeth's true love? Many who knew Elizabeth said he was.

PLOTS AGAINST THE Queen

Elizabeth's cousin Mary Stuart was queen of Scotland. In 1567, Protestant nobles in Scotland rebelled against Queen Mary. Mary fled to England, leaving behind her young son, James VI.

For nearly 17 years, Mary stayed in England under the watchful eyes of Elizabeth's guards. Elizabeth knew that Mary might try to overthrow her. Mary had the support of local Catholics, who believed she was the rightful queen of England. Because Elizabeth's parents' marriage was annulled, some felt she had no claim to the throne. Mary agreed with her supporters and plotted against her cousin. When the plot failed, Elizabeth had to decide Mary's fate. She did not want to behead the former queen of Scotland. Yet she was afraid Mary would continue to plot against her.

Her fears proved true. Anthony Babington was a rich, young Londoner and a member of a secret group of Catholics. In 1586, he planned to kill Elizabeth and make Mary the queen. Babington's plot was discovered, and he was executed. This time Elizabeth's councilors convinced her that Mary was too dangerous. Elizabeth was forced to make a choice. She signed Mary's death warrant. In February 1587, Elizabeth's cousin was put to death.

Elizabeth signed a death warrant ordering the execution of her cousin Mary Stuart.

Another threat to Elizabeth's crown came in 1588. King Philip II of Spain plotted to invade England and take the crown for himself. Philip had been married to Elizabeth's older sister, Mary. He believed that gave him the right to the throne. Philip wanted England to become a Catholic country again. He also planned to secure safe travel for his ships. English sailors attacked the ships as they carried gold and silver from the New World.

The Spanish king assembled a mighty fleet of 130 ships, 20,000 soldiers, and 8,000 sailors. The ships left Lisbon and headed into the English Channel. The English sent out a smaller fleet, but their ships had an advantage. Their cannons could shoot over a longer distance. On July 28, after nine hours of fighting, the Spanish ships headed for home. On the way, several storms devastated the Spanish **armada**. Less than half of the fleet made it back to Spain. All the English ships sailed safely home.

English sailors lit ships on fire before sailing them toward their Spanish enemies.

armada — a large group of warships

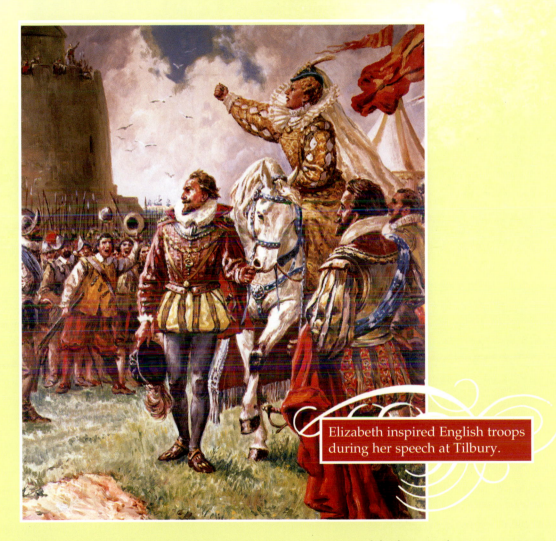

Elizabeth inspired English troops during her speech at Tilbury.

While the ships battled at sea, an army was assembled near the town of Tilbury. There Elizabeth made one of her greatest speeches. Dressed all in white and sitting atop a white horse, Elizabeth united her troops. She told the soldiers she was ready to fight alongside them to protect her kingdom.

Elizabeth's
LAST DAYS

The winter of 1602 saw Elizabeth's health fading. She had a cold but refused medicine. Sweets she normally enjoyed went uneaten. The palace mirrors were covered so she wouldn't have to look at her worn face. Her face heavily powdered, Elizabeth tried to keep up her queenly appearance. She may have been ill, but she insisted on wearing fancy gowns and jewels. Her most important jewel, her coronation ring, could no longer be worn. Elizabeth hadn't removed the ring since she was 25 years old. It had grown into her flesh and had to be cut off her finger.

By March 1603, Elizabeth was too weak to stand. On the morning of March 24, the 69-year-old queen took her last breath. She may have died from blood poisoning, cancer, or simply old age. Thousands grieved for their ruler as they watched the funeral procession. Queen Elizabeth I was buried at Westminster Abbey where she had been crowned 45 years earlier.

A horseman waiting in the courtyard galloped north to Scotland with the news. Had she lived, Queen Mary Stuart might have gotten her wish to rule England. Instead, her son was crowned King James I.

Members of the royal court were saddened by Elizabeth's illness and death.

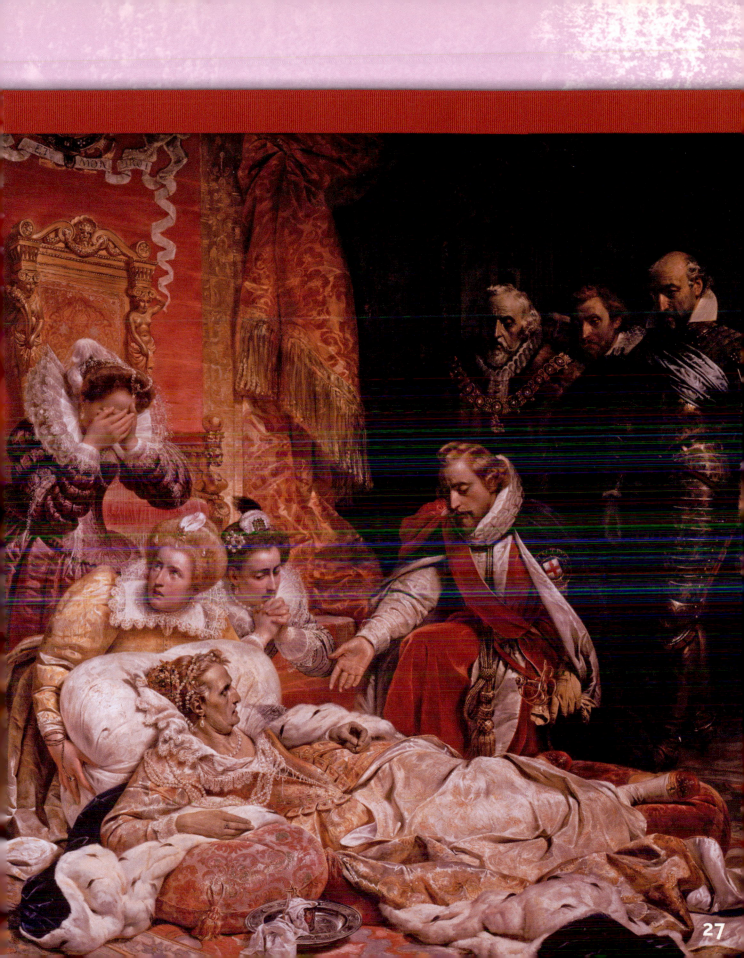

GOOD QUEEN BESS

Queen Elizabeth I brought the people of her small nation together, and England prospered. Merchants, tradesmen, and craftsmen thrived. Trade ships carried English goods to other countries. Adventurers explored the New World of the Americas. Painters, poets, and writers were welcomed in court. Her long rule came to be called the Elizabethan Age.

Elizabeth had great compassion for the common folk. Her crown, she realized, depended on their good will. Her loyalty was returned with affection and earned her the nickname "Good Queen Bess."

Some people still think Queen Elizabeth I is one of the greatest rulers who ever lived.

Glossary

annul (uh-NULL) — to cancel or end legally

armada (ar-MAH-duh) — a large group of warships

Catholic (KATH-uh-lik) — a member of the Roman Catholic Church

coronation (kor-uh-NAY-shun) — the ceremony in which a king or queen is crowned

heir (AIR) — someone who will become king or queen when the current ruler dies

heretic (HAIR-uh-tic) — a person whose actions or opinions are different from those of a particular religion or unacceptable to people of authority

Parliament (PAR-luh-muhnt) — the group of people who have been elected to make the laws in England

Protestant (PROT-uh-stuhnt) — a Christian who does not belong to the Roman Catholic or Orthodox Church

revolt (ri-VOHLT) — a fight against a government or an authority

smallpox (SMAWL-poks) — a disease that spreads easily from person to person, causing chills, fever, and pimples that scar

treason (TREE-zuhn) — the act of betraying one's country

Read More

Adams, Simon. *Elizabeth I: The Outcast Who Became England's Queen.* World History Biographies. Washington, D.C.: National Geographic, 2005.

Bingham, Jane. *Elizabeth I.* Great Women Leaders. Chicago: Raintree, 2009.

Riley, Gail Blasser. *Tower of London: England's Ghostly Castle.* Castles, Palaces, and Tombs. New York: Bearport, 2007.

Internet Sites

FactHound offers a safe, fun way to find educator-approved Internet sites related to this book.

Here's what you do:

1. Visit *www.facthound.com*
2. Choose your grade level.
3. Begin your search.

This book's ID number is 9781429623117.

FactHound will fetch the best sites for you!

Index